CW01522694

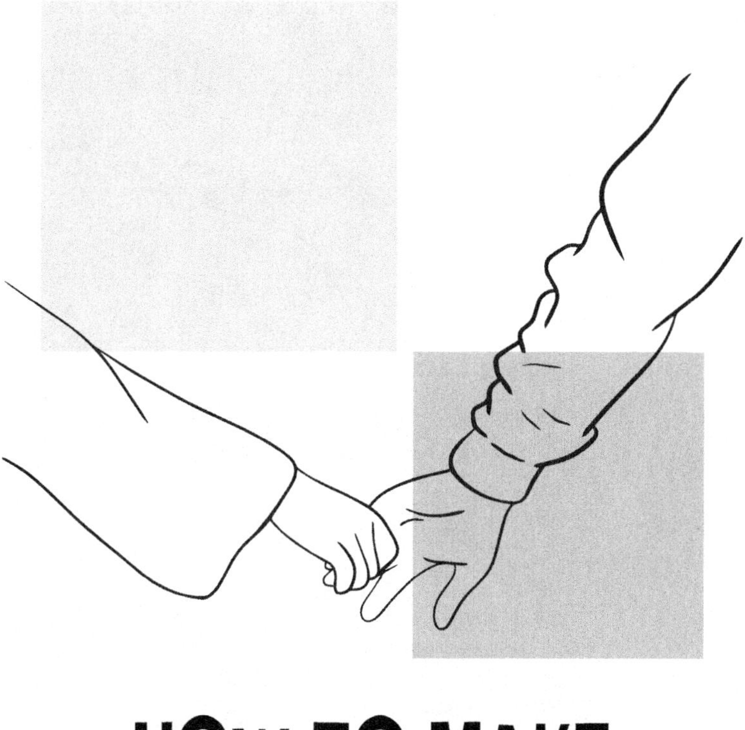

HOW TO MAKE YOUR GIRLFRIEND HAPPY

Relationships are a lot of work, but they can also be incredibly fun and rewarding. While you can't actually make another person happy, with a little effort and basic kindness you can help give your girlfriend what she needs to find joy in your relationship. You'll need to get to know your girlfriend as an individual and figure out what she needs, wants, and values. It's also important to be supportive and treat her respectfully, and to look for ways to keep the relationship exciting and fun.

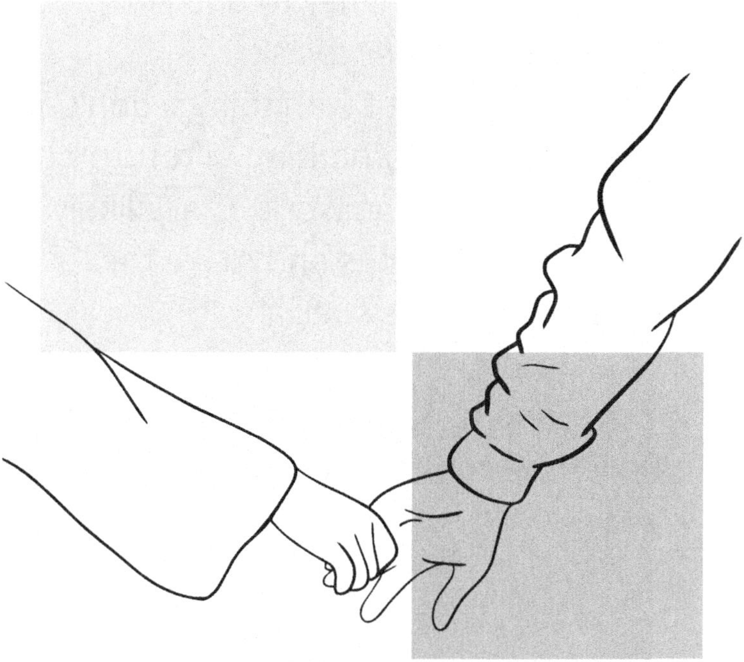

METHOD 1
MAKING HER FEEL
GOOD

Offer to help her with things. Lending a helping hand is a great way to show your girlfriend how much you care about her and help her feel special. Offer to pitch in without waiting for her to ask.

- When you help out with things, don't act like you expect something in return or complain about the work. That's likely to lead to hard feelings and make the gesture seem less special.
- For example, you might say, "Hey, you've been working hard all day. Why don't you let me cook dinner tonight?"

Give her gifts from time to time. Brighten your girlfriend's day and show her you're thinking of her by giving her a gift now and then. It can be for a special occasion, when she's feeling down, or just because. Don't worry about blowing a lot of money on anything fancy—she'll likely appreciate the gesture, even if it's something small or simple.

- The gifts you get will feel more meaningful if they connect to who she is as a person or what makes your relationship special. For example, you might print out and frame a nice picture of the two of you or buy her a mug with her favorite quote on it.
- When you give her the gift, say something like, "I saw this and thought of you!"

Schedule quality time with her. Spending regular one-on-one time with your girlfriend is one of the best ways to deepen your bond with her and help her feel loved. Try to schedule a date night or some other special time together for just the two of you at least once a week.

- For example, you might have dinner and a movie, go for a walk together, or just hang out at home together and play video games.
- Take turns choosing what you do during your time together. Letting her call the shots sometimes will show that you value her wants and needs.

Show her physical affection. Physical touch is an important part of a romantic relationship for most people. Show affection for your girlfriend by holding hands, hugging, kissing, or giving her a backrub. Just make sure you ask her what she's comfortable with and respect her wishes if she doesn't want to be touched!

- Sex is an important part of a healthy relationship for many couples, but try to incorporate physical touch that isn't sexual. Your girlfriend will likely feel more comfortable—and enjoy your intimate moments more—if your kisses and hugs don't always come with strings attached!

Say nice things to her. Everyone likes to hear kind and supportive words from their partner. Saying positive things to your girlfriend will help her feel loved and appreciated, which will improve your relationship overall. So, if you're thinking something nice about her, don't keep it to yourself—say it out loud!

- Try a classic "I love you," or say other things to let her know how you feel about her. For example, "You brighten my whole day," or "I'm so happy when we're together."
- You can also try giving her compliments, like, "You were awesome in class today!" or "Your eyes are just so gorgeous."
- Use words to express gratitude or appreciation, too. Say things like, "Thanks so much for coming to my recital. You're the best!"

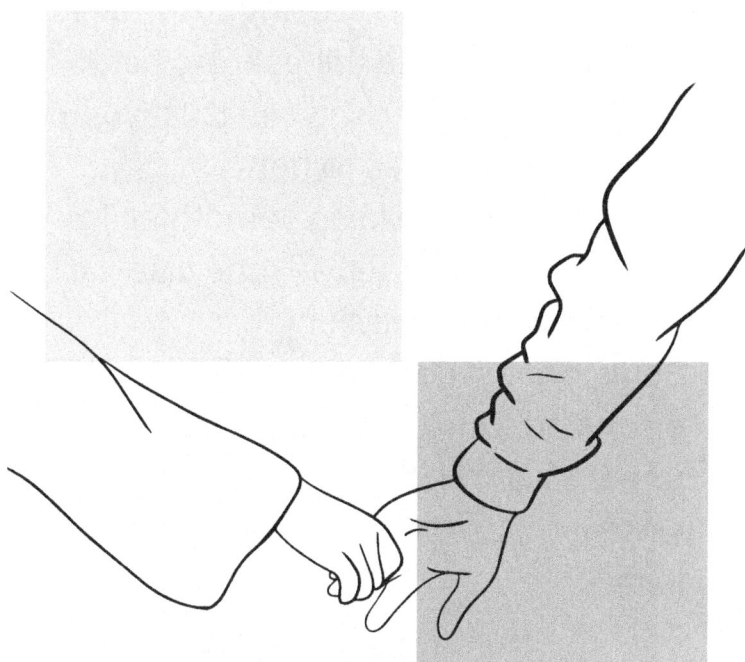

METHOD 2
BEING A LOVING
AND SUPPORTIVE
PARTNER

Sevecondey

Be honest and trustworthy with your girlfriend. The best relationships are built on honesty and trust. Show your girlfriend she can count on you by being truthful—don't lie to her or hide things from her. Additionally, show her she can trust you by keeping your promises to her.

- If she asks you to keep something in confidence, don't tell anyone else without her permission!
- Being honest doesn't mean being rude or unkind. Don't say things that are unnecessarily harsh or mean and try to write it off as "brutal honesty" or "tough love."

Keep your behavior kind and respectful. This may seem like basic common sense, but your girlfriend will be happiest if you treat her with compassion and respect. This means not only being there for her and doing nice things for her, but also respecting her boundaries, listening to what she has to say, and apologizing when you mess up. You can also be respectful by:

- Not yelling at your girlfriend, calling her names, or talking down to her.
- Treating her as an equal.
- Respecting her wishes if she asks you to stop doing something.
- Standing up for her if you see other people being disrespectful.
- Giving her space and allowing her to have time to herself or with other friends.

Let her know you are there when she needs you. To make your relationship with your girlfriend fulfilling and happy, do your best to be supportive in both good and bad times. That means not only being there to comfort her when she's down, but also celebrating with her when things are going well.

- Be her cheerleader when she's going through challenges. Congratulate her and tell her how proud you are when she accomplishes her goals.
- When she's having a tough time, be there to support her with both words and actions. Ask her if there's anything you can do to help.

Listen actively when she wants to talk. Good communication will make your relationship run more smoothly and help both of you stay happy. If your girlfriend has something to say to you, give her your full attention and listen without interrupting. Let her know that what she has to say is important to you and that you really want to hear and understand her.

- Put your phone away when she talks to you. Make eye contact, nod, and use verbal cues (like "Uh huh," or "I see") to let her know you are listening. Ask questions or rephrase what she says to make sure you understand.
- Resist the urge to offer advice unless she asks for it.
- Likewise, don't be afraid to open up to her and talk about your own feelings. She'll understand where you're coming from better if you're willing to be vulnerable.

Own up to your mistakes. Everyone messes up sometimes. If you make a mistake in your relationship, your girlfriend may be disappointed, sad, or angry with you. When this happens, resist the urge to point fingers or get defensive. Simply acknowledge that you messed up and offer a sincere apology.

- When you apologize, take full responsibility for your own feelings and actions. Don't use language that puts the blame on your girlfriend.
- For example, don't say things like, "I'm sorry you're so upset, but I wouldn't have yelled if you weren't always late." Instead, try something like, "I'm sorry, I shouldn't have yelled at you like that. I was frustrated, but that wasn't a good way for me to react."
- If you do want to address your girlfriend's behavior, use "I" language that focuses on how you feel instead of sounding accusatory. For example, "When you're late, I feel like my time isn't that important to you."

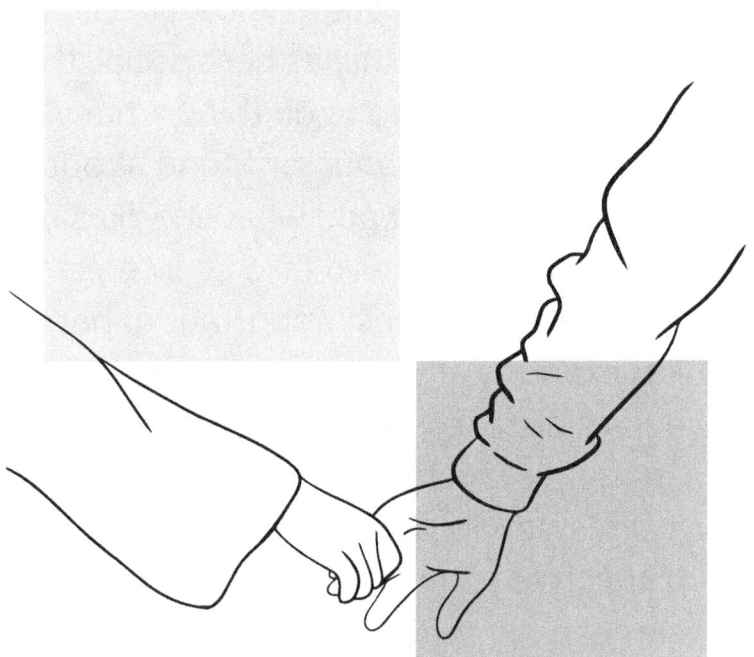

METHOD 3 UNDERSTANDING WHAT MAKES HER HAPPY

Sevecondey
Ediciónes

Take time to learn about your girlfriend's interests. Your girlfriend is an individual with her own hopes, fears, wants, and needs. The more you get to know about who she is and what makes her special, the easier it will be for you to do things that bring her joy. Talk to your girlfriend about what she cares about and what she likes to do. Try to participate and take an interest in the things that are most important to her.

- For example, if your girlfriend says she enjoys playing video games, ask her about her favorites. See if she's interested in playing games with you.
- If she likes to write, ask if you can read some of her work.

Communicate with her about what she wants and needs. It will be hard to know what your girlfriend wants from your relationship unless you ask her. Checking in with your girlfriend will not only let her know you care about her, but will also make it easier for you to be supportive. Encourage her to speak up if she needs something, and ask her simple questions like:

- "What would you like to do today?"
- "Is there anything I can do to help?"
- "Do you want to talk about it?"
- "Are you having fun?"

Avoid making assumptions about your girlfriend. Assumptions can be very damaging in relationships. Don't fall into common pitfalls by assuming that you know what your girlfriend feels, thinks, or wants. When in doubt, always ask!

- Don't assume your girlfriend knows what you're thinking or feeling, either. If something's on your mind, open up to her in a loving and respectful way.
- For example, don't assume she enjoys watching romance movies just because it's "a girl thing." You might find out that her ideal date is going to the zoo or doing a game night at the pub, instead.
- Don't just assume she's happy in the relationship, either. Check in with her occasionally and ask for feedback. For example, you might say, "Hey, would you like it if we went out for dinner more often?"

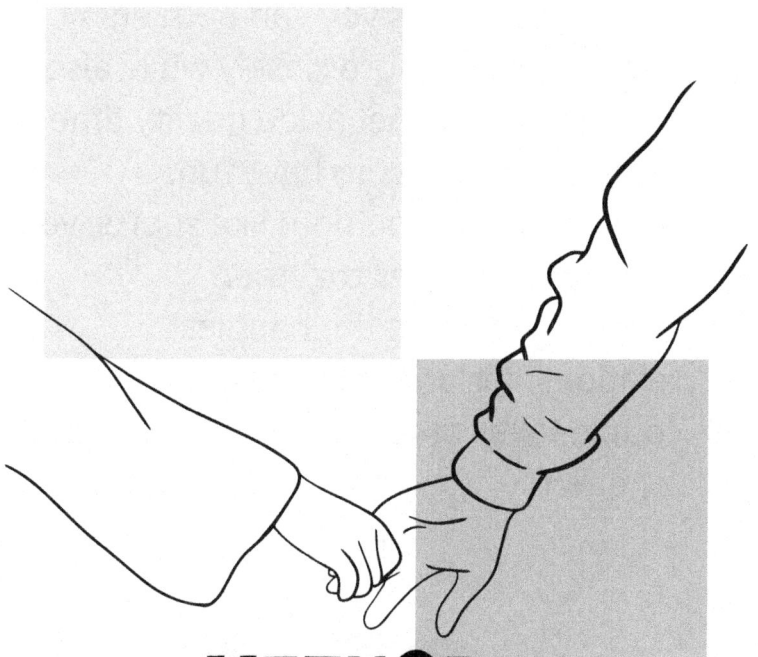

METHOD 4
KEEPING THE
RELATIONSHIP
EXCITING AND FUN

Sevecondey

Spend time together doing things you both enjoy. Having fun together is a great way to keep the relationship positive for both of you. Finding activities you can both enjoy will help you bond more closely while also having a good time. Set aside quality time for the two of you just to have fun.

- For example, if you both like sports, you might go to games together.
- Studies show that the happiest relationships are those where the couple takes time to play and have fun together!

Try new experiences together. In addition to doing things you already know you both like, you can keep your relationship exciting by getting outside your comfort zone together and trying new things. This will help you and your girlfriend create strong memories together and help keep the spark in your relationship alive.

- For example, you might travel to a new place together, take a class together on a topic you're both curious about, or pick up a new mutual hobby.

Get to know her friends and family. Your girlfriend will be happiest if her other relationships continue to thrive while you're together. By taking an interest in her friends and family, you can show her that you respect the importance of that part of her life. Plus, it's a way for the two of you to have fun and socialize together! Try to make time to do things together as a group instead of just hanging out with your girlfriend one-on-one all the time.

- Likewise, introduce your girlfriend to your own friends and family. Try to include her sometimes when you spend time with them.

Surprise her occasionally with something romantic or fun. Planning time together is important, but the occasional surprise can also help keep things exciting. Plan a mystery date, give her an unexpected gift "just because," or surprise her by cooking her favorite dessert.

- Don't worry about making your surprise elaborate. It could be something as simple as leaving a little love note somewhere for her to find.

Go out of your way to make her feel special. We all have a deep need to feel special. A lot of relationships start to sputter when one or both partners stop making the other feel like they're number one, so ask yourself how you can make your partner feel significant, appreciated, and loved today. For instance, tell your girlfriend she's beautiful, or send her a flirty text message or a message telling her you're thinking of her.

Printed in Dunstable, United Kingdom